PRINCE
OF
THORNS

Book 1 of the Luciferian Chronicles

REDA ISSA

authorHOUSE®

AuthorHouse™ UK
1663 Liberty Drive
Bloomington, IN 47403 USA
www.authorhouse.co.uk
Phone: UK TFN: 0800 0148641 (Toll Free inside the UK)
UK Local: (02) 0369 56322 (+44 20 3695 6322 from outside the UK)

Published by AuthorHouse 02/09/2022

ISBN: 978-1-6655-9112-6 (sc)
ISBN: 978-1-6655-9113-3 (e)

Print information available on the last page.

Any people depicted in stock imagery provided by Getty Images are models, and such images are being used for illustrative purposes only. Certain stock imagery © Getty Images.

This book is printed on acid-free paper.

CONTENTS

THE SURFACE

The surface comes to light
the surface is light surprised!
Where the sun shines
each surface carries
its own world down below
kind of like the tip of every iceberg that floats passed.
it hides the ill darkness
of that which is below
as kingdoms do with their lesser republics.
Luciferous is the forbidden kingdom
Beirut her capital republic
and her memory belongs to the light on the surface.

Xenophon the dreamer of the west romanticises
finding light in the east,

then says to his self with conviction
that
'Enlightenment is lost to light
Enlightenment is of a different shade
the unrecognised shade
(And then the light of reality's menacing sun fades…)

Enlightenment is the light that has a deal with down
below
That which is dark
it is the light which races with circular spaces
that are blank
the spaces the cosmos like to forget to take
because the light is fake!
Light are just repeated copies of enlightenment
and the kingdom has been led astray
into making mistake after mistake
for light to make its mark in ether...
and the mob then calls it civilised!'

Surfaces are always a success
That type of success
Which gives wings to light
which is blessed in return.

A lonely space
it is indeed
to be at the top of civility
for,
yes! Civilisation embraces
The faces
Of each other,
embraces light,

however random
or alien from me and from you
it is the magic that manages to connect the two
but civilisations have cut off's
to underworlds
because the promise between civility and the wild
was never a guarantee
I, Xenophon, guesses…

When in the wild the gift of tomorrow is borrowed
from the sorrow
that was yesterday
and civilisation then erects walls of trauma
and has archers on the walls
ready to fire arrows from weapons upon
whichever individual civilisation deems as a demon.

Behind the great divide
The trauma
that falls off from the top of the steep archer tower
a new world awaits
outside
one different than inside the gates
inside the forbidden kingdom'

Xenophon fantasies imaginations of a different world
and is set on trying
to understand the indifference

of the two shades:
enlightenment and light
and walks into the darkness with a light
to inspect,

Indeed, darkness can only be examined by light!

THE FORBIDDEN KINGDOM

And the answer to the riddle
between East and West
Enlightenment and light
is a riddle itself
it is a riddle decorated
intoxicated with awesome expensive jewels and
wonders
shrouded in gold,

but what is the riddle to
The fall of the fragmented
Empire the fall of Orentis, now a Forbidden Kingdom
turned into Luciferous, whose capital is Beirut.

MAP OF BEIRUT

THE LEPER KING

(Present Time)

It is late at night
In the hours
When all inside the palace are asleep
When all in this failed kingdom are asleep
that Salazar the Evil
Then
Stares into his mirror and speaks

'No birds sing
For Leper kings,'
(As the pupil in his eyes dilate due to rubbing his
medallion)
He continues to say
In his juvenile way

'Just ravens
Who crow
At night
in the moments before day has fully turned into night
In the hours when the moon
Takes up the centre stage
Of one's view into the incredible night sky,'

Salazar goes on to rub
His heavy medallion
wrapped eloquently around his neck,

Which makes him feel important
which gives him the false feeling of feeling intent and
competent
for wearing the cerebrum mineral
this element made of titanium3 which guarantees
the wearer
everlasting life
which grants immortality,
for its algorithmic property made by the mixing of
telomerase,
the cell of the soul, with titanium
which together form mineral as strong as titanium
steel, and as light as a feather,
and
which prolongs life by the mixing
of the cells of the soul with body cells,
which make age and mortality a thing of the past.

and this King
refuses to share this mineral with the other great
families of the kingdom
and taxes them
millions of Damiani's (the currency used in the
kingdom and that is used in Beirut).

From his own great greed of hoarding this medallion
and mines
a medallion which establishes everlasting life
and allows him to horde in immense wealth from
mines,
whose side-effects intoxicates the wearer
mentally with cruelty and greed,
which Salazar has the remotest idea of.

This reward
this gift to life
Unjustly served with in the kingdom
harrowed by taxes
so that the miracle of Cerebrum is kept by
the king and him alone.

And Salazar defiantly says to himself
'My God how many men have reached
such heights
Before realising their time has come
Haha!
But not mine!
Not mine!'

The worried evil king
Looks into his decaying face
His once handsome face
And says to himself

'My power is almost absolute,
angels are resolute under me,
but
There is this tiny problem
of
the prophecy
which deem him
Xenophon
my nephew
as the heir
to the throne
and the true wearer of this mineral
said to be the sharer of Cerebrum
to all within this Kingdom
ha-ha to the throne that I sit upon!

this idol
my nephew
the son
of my legendary older Brother
Hector II
my father's favourite
the people's favourite.

and I his acting Regent
falsely killing his father
to become the handsome one
Since I am second born!

But I can't kill him,
I can't kill Xenophon
As I did his father

Not while my younger brother
Is kept alive!
and is in on the secret....'

Salazar comforts himself
by staring into the cerebrum upon the medallion
with eyes transfixed on its greed
he then nervously says to himself

'Ah
The entitlement
that power brings
And the people I tax and rule
have no idea
that I steal their mineral
let alone that I usurped the Throne or stole
What is mine!
the mine is mine
and
Why shouldn't I control it
why shouldn't I tax the people!

with worried tears in his eyes
he speaks

'But
the Prince is no more young
but I can keep him ignorant of his power
distract him
give him a harlot,
use our great wealth to buy him toys
but how can I change his heart?
I have found immortality
yet not love!

how can I manipulate and control him
there is also the option of murder
….
my younger brother though is too close to him
It will turn the kingdom against me
it's a big ask
big ask with a simple answer'….

Salazar anxiously justifies to himself
'I have made sure
The mine runs
made sure that I am immortal!'

Salazar takes of the golden halo
Placed in the centre table
And then wears it.

To himself he jealously says
'This golden chalice
That cradles the responsibility
and lives of the many people who live in this kingdom
is what this halo symbolises,
like those that hovers over the heads of angles
but intercepted by gravity
it sits on my head as the wearer,
was it not meant to be enjoyed as an accolade?
A golden monolith of wisdom,
Yet to wear this crown is meant to be an honour
an honour to the self, an honour to the King to be
enjoyed by the King!'

Salazar continues to repeatedly think
'How did
my legendary brother Hector II,
he not only loved by everyone.
but also worshipped by everyone?
As a true king
A king worthy of his title
As King of Luciferous!
A king! (stops)
….
Yet
yet,
We are of the same blood
(Salazar reassures himself)

My brother Hector and I
The same
yet I never had the grace
to strike wonder in the eyes of people,
so, I
I
I just took his place'
as the flash of the titanium then flickers in his eyes.

Xenophon is kept inside
And has no knowledge of how life is outside the
palace doors
of the forbidden kingdom
Or any idea of how life was in the Golden Age of his
father's reign
the Golden reign of Hector and Mayar,
(he was told that they died in an accident since he
was young)

No knowledge of the civil war which broke out in
the kingdom
to have been kept by marriage of
his father's family,
Salazar's family
known as the Damiani's
because of their hold on the titanium mines
And mothers' family the Dahabieh or 'the Gold'
because of their control over the kingdom's gold mines.

The riddle to finding of this precious stone
this mineral Cerebrum
and the change in currency from Lira into Damiani's
was found by Hector I, father of both Hector II and
Salazar.

before the marriage of Hector II of house Damiani
to Mayar of Dahabieh
These two wealthiest houses of the realm were at
peace,
house Damiani from the south and house Dahabieh
from the north
and the wedding of Hector II to the beautiful Mayar
was the talk throughout the kingdom
celebrated by 101 days of festivity as ordered by King
Hector I
for his heir Hector II.
Xenophon
Prince and heir
to the throne
never new of this Peace
peace that almost seemed utopian
better yet the existence of a place called
Orentis
which was the kingdom's name before it was thrown
the curse
that is Luciferous.

The kingdom in motion
on a lie
and Xenophon just living life as he always did
Not understanding that Luciferous
Is the produce of the curse
A curse that was started
even before
his father was murdered by his best friend and brother
Salazar
The Unjust king
The King of chaos
and that he was the prophesied child
to bring peace to the land!

War broke out when the mineral Cerebrum was
found
between the two families
and peace was established together
but it was shortly kept!
it was short for the heavy murder of the king Hector II
by the devilish hands of his brother Salazar
who always wins by turning his back to the light of
equality.

Orentis was not the cursed land of Luciferous that it
is today.

Now,
with this Leper regent king taking control at the wheel
the devil
has been able to repaint our Lands red
Red with the blood of the kingdom's best people
And cursed those people into the darkness of these
lands
to live with the spell
That is Luciferous
Which has slowly and gradually cast the people to hell.

Union was established
by the coming together of the two warring families
that of Damiani's my father's prestigious line
And by that of Dahabieh, my mother's noble
admirable and charismatic line
By which Xenophon, is the product of.

A guard dressed in green then informs the imposter
king that
Xenophon is fast asleep
and with that,
the King creeps into his bed
then
stares from his leper eyes

Through the dome
And into the starless night sky
He likes to think that the bright lights in the cosmos
are circulating in motion
through the palace's glass dome
that there are in fact stars there
But with greedy Salazar stars don't exist,
Except for one,
himself
(Sixteen years before, at the time of the finding of
the mines Naval Commander Adonys, the youngest
member of the Royal guard and the youngest uncle of
Xenophon, gives a speech at the Phoenix auditorium,
in a conference known as the Concert of Phoenixes.)

CONCERT OF PHOENIXES

(18 years before)

'My fellow delegates
Representing capitals from left and right
Across the lands of Orentis
From East to West!
we are gathered here today
To discuss the one fate of humanity
after the passing of my Great brother Hector II
to discuss
the fate of our mine which can either hold the
fates of our ruin or the fates of our prosperity,
for the discovery of the mineral Cerebrum
can bring balance to our kingdom
to Orentis
a land that is filled with wonder and bliss.

This canny mineral which connects the circle of
Birth and Rebirth
we give thanks to our mine
whose presence promises to hold our whole kingdom
and the world
In balance!

Keeping the economy of society intact
keeping the very fate of Orentis' world

Intact
The fate that balanced
Light with shadow.

After the passing of the great Hector II
who gave his life for us,
this mineral for us all to share
In view of stellar order
and power
Held by the mine
to fund a war
in
Beirut
a land where justice walks with injustice
Because of the Phoenixes spell
Which Condemns people
To burn out then come out
as phoenixes there after!
Are we now tasked with solving this problem!
A problem whose answer that will be justice
for our kingdom!
and certainly, appears to make the future look set for
centuries,
(with excitement in his voice, Adonys says)
'Finally, what is injustice today, will turn into justice
tomorrow
by the finding of the mineral Cerebrum.

Never has so much depended on the decision
that
We make today
that we make together
From this very conference this concert of delegates
and Inside the Colosseum of Phoenixes
We are gathered to answer the cursed spell
Of dying and becoming reborn
The spell which spells
That we must be condemned to hell
and its fiery cauldron before
we are freed into its turquoise well
A well of immortality
Death is gone and no more
Life triumphs'

says flamboyant Adonys, speaker of the guards and
youngest brother to king Hector II from the royal
family Damiani!

PRINCE OF THORNS

(Present Time)

(Down in the sheltered palace)

Xenophon goofily wears his uncles' incredible golden halo and imagines himself one day reigning with a crown upon his head just as his incredible uncle who he will come to greatly detest does.

And since according to tradition of succession the crown must pass to him, his father after all is the one true king tragically murdered by the people, the people of Luciferous whose capital is Beirut!

Then the King, Salazar I, steps in.

'See oh mighty uncle, the crown does look nice on me. Do you not wish for me to run your mines and produce more of the silver coin, (the nickname of Cerebrum) and hope that that will be enough to silence the complicated people complaining down in the valley, which is what you do right?'

To himself Xenophon innocently questions,
'Those whom I have never seen or been kept away from all for my own safety, which after being shut

away for eighteen years, has conspired to turn me into a very frustrated individual.

'Get of the throne this instant, and how dare you wear my golden crown! Guards kindly (with every pun of irony intended) escort my nephew away from the Throne Room'
commands Salazar.
One of the guards is Adonys, Xenophon's favourite uncle.

'Are you ready for your name day tomorrow XO (Xenophon's nickname)' says Adonys, Xenophon's uncle and head of command to the Guards of the Circle of the Phoenix

With intrigue and fascination not to say without childish exhilaration young Xenophon of eighteen, says to the ears of Adonys as he is taken away
'I cannot wait for it!'
Indeed, this is very exciting, he will be named king and experiencing the city of love of which he, Xenophon has only ever heard great stories about or seen great pictures of!'

With all that said and done
Xenophon produces a smile despite being forcibly dragged and carried away by orders of his cowardly uncle.

To himself he thinks

There is much to hope for tomorrow, but fear wraps itself as a bubble where hope exists but hope from idea and isolation and without experiencing the cities magic.

Later he and upon reflecting

He then spectacularly realises

that hope is only one side of the coin,

experiencing hope is the coin's other side,

and the other side is a completely different game.

Xenophon says to himself 'I am ready to walk into Beirut, hopefully though not as a warrior that must fight gladiators in an arena of envy, according to what his uncle says, as Xenophon romanticises:

'Xenophon the people are envious, they killed your father and will do the same to you!'

but I will instead walk through Beirut with poetry and song., I am your regent protector!'

I want to come in as this Prince of Music, singing with people, hoping to restrike the solid chord between people and monarchy.

.

To himself he says

'Tomorrow it will all change, I will go to the people as nephew to the man they all love. Love! Love! That's what the city is known for. Tomorrow I experience the movie apart from just seeing its incredible pictures, and this is all done without knowledge from my great and mighty uncle, Salazar I, how mad he will be to learn of this treachery, in fact how impressed will he be by me when I make history, and rectify the chord struck between people and the sword of 'Monarchy' when I go into Beirut?

Tomorrow I pierce the bubble that fear has wrapped its robes with

I learn of this spell that makes the Sultan of Swords dance so elegantly and immortally in hell.

THE BROKEN RECORD

In the room
the forbidden one in the west wing
with a barred entry
(Created since Xenophon was born)
said to have hosted kings
and welcomed all the great families
where all great decisions are made
to spin the world.

Xenophon examines the door then chooses to go in.

He notices cobwebs in the corners of the room
and an abandoned table with chairs
to his left it is a sword
and underneath it a piano
said to command the musical chords
of the howling winds outside.

The magic of striking the chords are so beautiful in
the palace
in the forbidden kingdom,
and give one the feeling that life is magical in Beirut,
a Broken ancient city
with all wonder and greatness
kept secret from Xenophon.

But Xenophon can't contain his excitement for tomorrow
'Tomorrow it will all change' he says.
For tomorrow is Xenophon's name day,
tomorrow Xeno (nickname) will go
to the theatre of dreams
of light,
but sees a half-torn list of records of all the kings that have ever served the kingdom
plastered in the walls of the west wing
and notices that the succession ended abruptly with King Hector I (Xenophon's uncle)
and anticipates that he will hear her screams instead.
With no ill intent on the current King that he loves he says
'Tomorrow I shall fix this broken record draped in the West Wing and animate the splendour of what was that room, when I make it mine, my own!'

Tomorrow has arrived!
It is August 4th and the year is 2020 AD
My name day is today!

The Coronation is today,
But the king has blocked its happening
blocked the light and magic of the moment.

Adonys comes in
'are you ready for a ride?'

I look upon the valley and hear the breeze sing a song
below the decorated balcony
beyond where there are rivers and streams.
It's early morning still,
in the hours when the old moon is yet to fade into
the new.
See how its pale light caresses the war-torn structures
around
Beirut, the mighty city
victim to sieges and traumas of countless wars
so, Adonys, my uncle who is also my tutor tells me.

War is a two-sided coin whose faces are against each
other,
But the civil war is over
It ended right before I was born
And into Beirut I go
the city which touches gravities root
the place where kings hear calls
and glide alongside the flights of Angels
from the Forbidden Kingdom
and as a beacon of light to shine into the dark
wilderness
which is away from the trouble of light
Into the darkness where the people apparently fight
And fight one another they do!

The sun is up:
I am going downtown
Down to the valley
Down to Beirut
to begin my day,
a glorious day
experience the magic
that is this city—
her buildings so pretty,
her songs so sad,
her birds gliding and chirping majestically
up above her streets of cobblestones

a city whose entry has been forbidden to me to see
and hear
how then can I lead?

Such a menacing city indeed.
the mirror
of a great civilization
at the great step between the East and West
so, my tutor Adonys says.

My uncle,
the king
Salazar I,
King Pangloss,
has kept me indoors,
saying it is for my best not to mix with the people—
they who killed my father,
according to him—
that it will be too traumatic
for me.

Now, I go down to Beirut
in search of the truth,
in search of the magic and Sage
of this city, which has a knack for absorbing
traumas and rage, countless times,
age after age,

with an ardent optimism for fixing
its broken record,
that my father could fix
and just by plugging in the missing pieces,
hoping to find and create peace
to harmonize the chord between the people and
monarchy

Only in a city as glorious as Beirut can one start the
curse that is Luciferous
Can one end the curse that is Luciferous!

THE IDENTITY OF THE LAST PHOENIX

Adonys takes Xenophon through an exit
From the Castle cave that only he knew existed
and the route passed Mayar statue
Where King Hector I touches her beak
a tunnel where the mines have run dry then proceeds
to says,
'Get ready to see the city of dreams, a city that creates
chaos and gives a name to tragedy,
one that your uncle has forbidden your eyes to see.
Welcome to Beirut! where its divine order invites
chaos,
afterall there is no order in chaos just a history of it.'
Adonys then looks at Xenophon and says
'You know who these people are?'
inquisitive Xenophon sensing a revelation about to
occur asks
'Hector I and the Phoenix Mayar as they are in 'the
Luciferous: A History book'
Adonys then says
'You don't know who they are?'
Xenophon closes his eyes and opens them
and after with intelligent suspicious eyes
sharply answers

'Those are my parents; I am the kingdom's heir, he born by the phoenix who will bring peace to the kingdom, untouched by the fires, as said in that chapter in the history book'

'Yes… they are your parents Xenophon'

says Adonys.

Angry emotions fill his inquisitive eyes of Xenophon as he says

'But my uncle Salazar said that both my father, his older brother, and my mother were killed in an accident, an accident perpetuated by the people of Beirut. And so, the crown passed to him as regent, too look after me until I become of age.'

Adonys corrects Xenophon, but changes with conviction and optimism, since he is talking to Xenophon, the latter who just found out that he was the just king. A king who just found out his identity of being the last Phoenix,

'That isn't how they died,' Adonys says bluntly.

'You are the last Phoenix Xenophon, yes, but in secret my brother the so-called King Salazar the Leper is planning to murder you once you are back in the kingdom and keep all power absolute for himself.

You are the promised the unburnt celestial who can bring peace to the kingdom and return it back to being as the rightful empire Orentis and Beirut the city of Enlightenment!

Back to days mixed with lightness and darkness'
Xenophon with shell shocked eyes, from the realisation upon learning his identity, rationalises that
'So you are telling me that my father and mother didn't die by accident nor by the hands of the people in Beirut, but was actually murdered, by Salazar and by his own hands?
Adonys with tears in his eyes looks up to the skies and says
'You know the night they died the world went into timeless mourning, years long. When my brother, my oldest brother, decided to adopt you and take you in. I was complicit, believing that it would be only for your advantage to be isolated and brought up by a king, though a false king, in a palace besides other lords, princes, and princesses. But upon the passing of your mother Mayar, the soul of Beirut was lost and thus the civil war ensued'.
Xenophon now in a calm rested manner and after connecting the dots with his starstruck eyes says
'Yes
so I don't need a regent I never did,
and what does this make him?
Not only childless but a liar a thief... a murderer!
that miszes and hordes
all the sweet gold from our opulent mines directly into his pockets.'

'Yes'

Xenophon still perplexed in understanding and never showing any spite
speaks
'Then why then didn't you take it; it was perfect for you! Why tell me this now?'
Adonys says in a serious tone
'Perfect? the world never owes you perfection.
Yes, I feel ashamed, I feel ashamed, but life is never perfect!
I was the youngest and last in the line of succession and as I said before I believed that the circumstances would have been in your favour,
and everyone in the Kings Guard is loyal to my tyrannical brother, and so it wouldn't be safe.
The kingdom isn't safe,
especially this murky cloud which covers Beirut,
the port blast and fog of War
whose clarity
and end
only you can bring.'

So they venture out, out to 'No Man's Land' to the empty concert hall,
Where Adonys leaves Xenophon
to meet a person
known to all in Beirut and outside the Kingdom

as 'The Singer', who actually is Mayar's brother, so
his uncle.
Saying to Xenophon before he leaves
the war-torn desolate theatre,
'No Man's Lands'
and says one last remark before leaving
'Remember this my Prince my King, know who you
are, and that the world never owed you perfection
'Bye bye!' a serious Xenophon says,
as this other handsome faced person known to Beirut
as the Singer
then enters the abandoned arena.

The identity of the singer is Meraxes the Gold
(Dahabieh). Meraxes an ancient name in Orentis,
and Gold for all for all his wealth,
who lives on the other side of the kingdom, and is
heir to everything on the other side.
He is Xenophon's uncle, his beautiful mother Mayar's
older brother.
Xenophon closes his eyes
and goes into the lampoons of imagination
and connects the dots
'Their marriage union was what held the two warring
sides together,
but since the murder of Xenophon's mother, the
angelic Phoenix Mayar and
father the charismatic chivalric King Hector II,

the union between our families and house has collapsed.
Thus, this dynastic war, that is eating up Beirut and
destroying the kingdom of Luciferous to its core.'

Maraxes turns away with that said
and a grave look takes over this man
this singer colloquially called 'Moughanie'
and sceptically
reads to his nephew

Ashburn Prophecy

From the ashes
of a world burned,
an angel is born
named Xenophon
and returned
to mend
a world torn in two
to rush to the rescue
with love
and arrives just in time to save the world from its chaos
and to restore order
as an inverse to this world that borders heaven and hell,
to broker with the joker of curse.
His birth is the verse of light sung in our darkest
universe
by both the mother and father.'

turns to his nephew Xenophon,
and says
'But Hector's heir
isn't dead,
the bloodline
the prophecy has not been spent.
At least that is what your uncle who risked his life to
bring you here,
what the brave Adonys has told us.

That all said I still don't believe you are who you say
you are'
Diligent Xenophon with even more fiery belief to
prove himself responds
'What would you have me do?'
As he looks at the pit of the immortal red and yellowish
ire, where the stage of the Amphitheatre used to be,
the very fire whose element is the algorithm that
makes the hybrid mineral Cerebrum
the mineral of immortality
and
Xenophon steps into the fire and walks out
unburnt.

'God almighty' as he bows down, and says
'You are the promised one,
the one to finish connecting the dots
and the one to redeem Luciferous back to greatness.'

With that said Xenophon then notices the true face
of the structures around him
yet remains surprisingly inquisitive and interested as
ever,
he is going to be the ruler of such lands,
this responsibility now belongs to him
the responsibility of redemption.

unphased by his setting
And with his shadow and that of the mountain
blocking light
The singer uncle ominously says
'we thought that the bloodlines of house Damiani
were all, but spent
the house forged by the marriage of the kingdom's
two great families
Dahabieh, my house and your mothers; and Damiani,
your father Hector II and the current tyrant on the
throne.
After my sister, Mayar's death, she who carried the
kingdoms soul
you,
the heart of the city died
with you the soul of Orentis
you are the true heart and heir
heir of not only the colosseum of Beirut but
the entire arena of the whole empire of Luciferous.'

'Moughanie' looks at Xenophon and says,
'We thought that our destined original Prince
had died with you
and all memory faded and died with it too
That romance and beauty between
Your father (the king Hecton II), the worthy the kind
the great, and mother (The beautiful Phoenix Mayar)
Had ended when they were killed
Killed by the King who acts as Regent with you

…

The sky dims and Moughanie proceeds to say

'But you are alive
the prophecy lives on
Beginning with the reign of your father King Hector,
and continued by you,
but your parents were killed just two years after you
were born
then
began jealous king Salazar's evil reign of terror
and the curse of the kingdom from being Orentis to
Luciferous.

The kingdom has since been condemned
to live in fear and error,
error from living in a curse

flowing from the verse sang by the lips of your uncle,
Salazar I
sketched on posters throughout his side of
West Beirut

Which poetically read

'Fight
fight in the light,
So that I may sleep in peace
and even in your dreams
amidst continuous screams
rise rise and fight again
and pray that the day will soon turn into night!'

As soon as the conversation ends
A thunderous noise occurs,
and shrapnel from the bomb nearly kills Moughanie,
but Xenophon's instantly throws his body over his
uncle, his mother's brother,
to protect him from the flames.

EXPLOSION IN BEIRUT

After absorbing this ominous
Water shedding conversation
Xenophon eccentrically exclaims with joy
'Hi ho Silver (petting his horse)
and mounts upon hissilver maned Horse ready
to see the important structures of Beirut,
a horse named Mynute
a name quipped by Adonys due to the fast speed in
which that horse travels by, which eventually became
his name.
That special horse is from the finest breed of horses,
Stemming from the ancient blood line as Incitatus,
which means swift,
For a murderous Roman emperor Caligula,
Not too unlike current king Salazar,
'I always suspected that he was perceived as a buffoon
who pounces around on the throne, so hated and
detested by the people'
'But a Murderer!?'

That realisation shocks Xenophon to his core,
Leaving him very winded as he goes to mount his
horse.

Mynute, who is the same age as Xenophon was given
to Xenophon as a present by Adonys when he himself
was just born being no older than a pup,
But Xenophon has never seen him until today.

The interesting part was how naturally and effortlessly
Xenophon mounts his horse
and as he heads back says

'Ah what a beautiful day
thank you uncle Adonys
The cosmos of the world
Are in motion
and the Mediterranean ocean is at play

As the party of two ride
continue to ride inside Beirut
Xenophon looks behind and notices that large iconic
cedar tree
underneath Palace balcony
so special it can be noticed even from far away
a tree of life that commands the magic of winds
and finds electricity in light for everyone.

or so he's am told
and that fountain underneath the mountains
where only this narcissistic king resides—

Adonys mounts upon his horse Zalfa also of the same breed,
in fact, born by the same mother horse, except a bit older and wiser than Mynute,
and says as they leave the theatre where they met the singer in person

'I will take you with me for a ride
on the wings of fallen kings
to where the angels in a choir sing
my prince

Ride down from mountains
to seas,
to the loud bustles of the city
amidst the breeze
that welcomes travellers of all sorts
at its ports.

All the swords of the world (metaphorically)
lay before
a stage,
this theatre for the souls
to dance and play.

Come with me:
follow me
to Beirut,

where magic from its fertile lands
no longer make seeds
that grow roses from burning fires,

where one could be one
with the pixies
that fly naively
above
with birds
and pass on
into the night sky.

Come with me:
hear Beirut
greedily laugh with her impressive society,
a city infamous for its charm.
Where you could
Drink wine straight from the red river streams.
Break bread with your neighbours.

Swim in the deeps of the Mediterranean Sea
whose saltwater's kiss the Luciferin shores,

where the people
always give more
and reciprocate with love

Xenophon excitedly trots behind
Adonys on their mission of espionage
And have just passed the fringes of the realm
Where Xenophon thought that the fertile land
of the palace stopped

How much hadn't he seen?

Of the city painted in pictures
A city which was once a city of electricity

Yet is also the capital of the Luciferian Kingdom
A city that no longer sparks like it used too

a city more... shocked and blown away
by the cracks and tears of the exploding dynamite,

Adonys and Xenophon are blown away
By the blast
And loose each other and can't make out each other's
silhouettes
From the residue of all that ash

'What happened?' Xenophon asks
'A horrible tragic thing young Xenophon.'
Says Adonys
'It is the crying of the new world begging the old one
to change,

Cries neglected by leaders of Luciferous
Who are led by my brother your uncle King Salazar!'

at that moment Adonys
Indeed, a loud explosion is the only music Xenophon
would be hearing
From this iconic day of August 4th.

Beirut a city whose spirit
and ambiance is more powerful than exploding
dynamite,
whose cracks and tears have just ripped the nation's
heart,
torn its people
apart from monarchy
apart from each other

the Irony is that
it's all in the same fertile land
Where power grows
From its plants
and commands where and when power ends.

Xenophon thinking to himself

'Though,
Karma is a witch!

Witches have memory when they cast in their spells
Spells which are summoned only for the traumatic
rise and falls of great empires.
But where is the rise of potential
only understood by the winds

What is justice for all?
but an idea of a through which all men sprint for.

For the magic of Justice only occurs in the truth of
originality in nature
not in the wilderness of thought.

And Ideas are only one side of the coin

And on the other side of the Coin of ideas
Is Beirut
The city left to grapple all the wonder and madness
from ages past and present.

In a nation held hostage and strangled
by the impressive wings
of negligent rule
By my uncle,
His Majesty, King Salazar I
Or should I say Pangloss I
The fool who thinks he knows what people should do.

Yet his injustices to the people
is not a fight between what's wrong and what's right—
it has never been!
But a person versus a people
It's the fight of injustice,
unbalanced and unfair before the light!
An injustice cloaked by the people
When they continue curse
By joining their king ins singing the Luciferin verse
and
Blanketed by a cloud of voices
from that explosion
that has rocked the empire's people
zero electricity
and still its people forever sing
sing of bringing down this imagined
world when the reality of our world
is that the true king
doesn't wear a crown
that is flipped upside down.'

instead, Salazar hides and acts like clown!

All the while in this dismal city,
this marvellous city—
that is a
playground for the privileged wealthy,
and a battlefield for the poor and needy.

having your uncle look over you
was fir the best
at the time atleast,
however, in light of the recent change in the state of
affairs in the kingdom,
the desperation of the people from
reckless taxing by the King
and his holdings of the Cerebrum,
who's algorithmic logic
is DNA code of your heart,
the heart of the Phoenix,
and the evil king doesn't have the code
to make more 'silver coins'
for that he needs you',

COBWEBS OF THE FUTURE

The explosion has happened
And the people
Leaderless lost to the wilderness of Luciferous
and left alone to pick things up,
abandoned by this narcissistic king
that the people accuse Salazar the stupid
for such Madness
and for neglecting our cries,
he who the people blame
for the port flames.

Xenophon is a man for the beauty of people
one who sees the beauty in a droplet
And not the greediness in an ocean.

So
he has gone up,
back to the palace,
Which stands unscathed
Before the burning of Beirut

The first place he goes to once in the palace
is
the forbidden room
and notices that

The fragile Cobwebs created as the bed
by that talented spider
Incredibly was untouched
and not destroyed…

Not destroyed?

How can something so frail
be so powerful in face of such destruction?

Zero is the number of death and rebirth.
Zero is the first number at the beginning of life, and
is also the last number when life has reached its end.

A PICTURE OF TWO

After the explosion

I bid farewell to Mouganie Dahabieh
my mother's brother
Whom I didn't know was my uncle until
Just now,
Andonys and I walk back to the palace
To grapple with this realisation
As heavy as the explosion
In Beirut, as she grapples hers

I walk into the palace
And for the first time
The palace appears to be different to me
The picture of two on the shelf
has
fallen on its face

A picture that I only realised until now
Was in fact a picture of my mother and my father
That picture of the famous two
The king and Phoenix
Were actually my parents, the Phoenix Mayar and
king Hector

Look at how peaceful everything looks
In the picture
Look at how happy they looked
Before
they departed and apparated into
another world

The world we are all destined to go to
But do our bests not to go too.

Yet you my father
You stand strong
You represent everything that isn't wrong
in our world.

Three days after the Ash simmers down
And after seeing the desolation of the people
Who ask
How can humanity rise up
That the Golden crown
In the picture that is on your head
That picture of both you and mum
In each other's arms
That picture of two
No longer belongs to you
And can't pass down through me
Not since your childless brother
Salazar

has wedged my succession
Not as protector which his title claims
But as a tyrant that leaves every
Track ablaze
Whose cruelty always
Makes him jump the Maze
The Maze everyone does to get to the top
To turn the wheel
the wheel only privileged to those at the top
to disastrously use as a mop
To wipe all memory of what was
Down at the bottom,

He is a usurper
A murderer
A thief
That Regent
Who keeps the crown
As a golden present
To himself
Using its power as fuel to feed into his cruelty,

But cruelty has no place in succession,
It can't have a place,
succession and cruelty
Whose magic
Are like the others poison
For cruelty he is immune to all

But one
And succession manifests all
But one
one is the others Achilles heel
And only one can turn the wheel

The Picture of two
Is all that remains pure
All that is left pure in the palace,
All of what's left in Luciferous
All that is pure in Beirut.

The picture of two
Is heavenly
a stark difference
From the dismal reality painted by life
Of a paradise
A paradise whose future is now lost
And gone
A paradise which has turned dystopian
By the very ashes
That would occur each time a hero is burned
A paradise seen through a hero's eyes
Is gone
Gone after you my king
After you my father
And after you my mother
fairest Phœnix

Our Phoenix Mayar
How can I lead
The recent infamous throne
And create a paradise for all in Luciferous
End the kingdoms curse
Which began due to your murderous deaths
and then restore the kingdom
back to the golden days of Orentis
where the kingdom rises and achieves with the sun
and sets in the west.

...

POWER SHARING

The explosion's cloud
Engulfs the entire city
Mouganie coils back
As a hermit crab to the safety of his side of East Beirut.

Xenophon is right beside him
processing all that he the prince has seen,
that he the lost heir to the throne of Luciferous has seen
Then juxtaposes it
with the mosaic of the chaos
just right outside the heavenly peace
and comfort of his palace
one thing he knows for sure is
the blast was the last straw
that pierced his bubble.

And with the desperation
of his entire nation
Mouganie says

'Pity the nation
Whose emptiness
Blows like the winds
That invites love in
To find its equation'.

Xenophon asks
'What do you mean?'

'Nephew
I mean
You are the solution to the equation
that you could be the bridge
The bridge in conscious
The bridge between the two warring families
Which have created a bipolar existence in Luciferous
Broken its melodic record and verse
Which binded together all its masses.
The problem with Luciferous was never other empires
The problem with it was Luciferous itself,
The people aren't one because of the person
Because of your uncle
Who murdered my sister, your mother Mayar,
and who murdered your father Hector II.'

Xenophon evades the question
But then pensively agrees and immediately knows
the answer
'Share the mine!
The mine which is run by a murderer
Whose substance miracle
is immortality for all
But selfishly kept for one
Salazar!

And his selfishness
is what has kept it away for all
and tarring it for all
Condemning all the people
Subjecting them to the monotonous and enharmonic
curse
that is Luciferous.

Xenophon to himself
No wonder there is frustration
This division between two sides
Has created a city where victims reside!
Turned the people into a mass of paranoia
Who then subject heroes to witch-hunt's
cruelly hounded by the masses,

But I am the phoenix
Xenophon the unburnt
And I will
turn all that is untuned and tragic
Into a melodic song of magic.
…
A different chord shall be struck by the lord
And from the ashes that burns heretic
I shall rise and strike the verses sung by Power
Power grows itself like a flower
Whose seeds make this nation bleed,

Xenophon answers his uncle Mouganie
'O pity the people!
Whose trouble
Was to repeat clearing out rubble
Whose leaders' fires are extinguished from
Loving the waters which put their fire out.'

Power is the curse which blankets all of Luciferous,
The curse that I must end.

A PLACID KING

Down from the palace
and in Beirut,
three days after the blast,
one desperate man cries out to the other less fortunate
    men behind him
as he takes his food rationing from the golden hot
    cauldron resting on charcoal embers to say:
'We are so hungry! We can barely amass enough
    food to feed ourselves, how can we even feed our
    children?'

Before the statue of our beloved Phoenix Mayar,
the people wait in dozens of never-ending lines
extending infinitely beyond.

Xenophon is in the line, back in Beirut
disguised,
wearing a plain grey
hooded cloak.

The people are hungry; the harmonizing chord
    between a king and his people has been broken.

But the people sing for their king,
surrounded by misery and terror in their desolate
    empty, squalor
down in Luciferous, which was once a paradise
where the King, my uncle, was loved by all.

Anger is burning up in the line. Tensions rise.
Waiting for hours for his turn, Xenophon pulls down
    his grey hoodie in front of the person rationing
    the meal. He gives his meal to the person behind
    him and leaves the line, without waiting for a
    thank you.

Upon the hill is where the castle sits.
Xenophon takes a secret route through the castle,
a route reserved for only the King and his family, who
    are known to the people as El Akhdar, meaning
    'Green', because of their wealth and the peculiar
    green-coloured eyes which the whole family of
    Damiani has.

Xenophon tells his childless uncle, the King
seated on his throne,
the King whose green eyes turn even darker with greed,
'My King, the people are frustrated to their limits!'

'Why didn't you go to the mine, where the future of
    this family lies?'
the King says, rubbing the silver medallion.

'I wanted to feel the desolation the masses felt.
I went down to see magic
and all that I saw was tragic!

The people are fed up. Yes, you were victorious with
my father'—Xenophon pauses and takes time—
'but you were never selfish. I've heard stories of
times of joy in Beirut,
times where you and my father, your younger brother,
would go down too and sing and play with the
same common man whose cries are now mere
whispers to you!'

Scowling and smirking, the King's eyes turn greener,
and to the leader of his guards, Adonys, Salazar says,
'You see what happens when I trust young people?
I assign Xenophon, my nephew, the simple task
of checking the productivity of our mine. Need
I remind you that the very same mine keeps
everything running on the hill. Instead you go
like the stupid boy that you are and stand in line
with the common folk.'

'They are the ones who put you where you are, and
they can take it back!'
exclaims Xenophon.

The guards draw Xenophon away from the King and
hands the King a report.
The King grabs the report majestically and points
his narrow dark-green eyes over it, then gives his
iconic smirk from the bottom of his lips and says,
'Thank you, Adonys. Give the orders to continue
rationing the people one meal per family each day.'

Xenophon is expelled from the meeting.

Right after Xenophon goes back out to the cliff and
before he retires to his bedchambers, he goes to
enjoy the fabulous, immersive, black night sky
and connect the dots
in the constellations of the waiting stars,
the stars which used to shine so brightly down on
the city of Beirut from the castle—
oh yes, the castle, which used to be an attraction but
now is only a fort
cut off from the rest of the world.

The meeting is finished.
Pangloss the King retires to his room,
takes off his golden crown,
and naively stares through the glass dome into
the same black night and sleeps on his greedy
memories which act as pillows to his conscience,

but he doesn't connect the constellations of the
    same stars as his nephew
as he rubs the silver medallion hanging from his neck
and then closes his greedy eyes
and dreams with his hand over heart of the heart of
    things that are already dead and goes to sleep with
    his cruel smile.
As a placid King ignorant from the suffering of his
    kingdom.

THE LEPER KING TWO (THE CROWN)

(The Next Day)

The Leper King Salazar takes off
His crown
Whose weight feels as light as a feather
And then looks curiously at this crown
Resting upon the table
With its Ornate with patterns
And beautiful designs

how
How could something so small
So, light
symbolise so much
And rule over so many

Bear the brunt of responsibility over
The entire Luciferian society.

The table is plain
Brown and smooth
Smooth as the surface of a pond
And it is given importance by the Luciferian crown
Placed in the middle of the already balanced table

A spectacle indeed
An object admired desired and so revered
(Salazar contemplates)

What a tragedy to the world
This world that I am a part of
For something to have so much control over so many
Only for this crown to be worn by me,
The usurper
Usurpers are an injustice to all
That are original

the skin eats itself off the Leper kings
Frightening face
a little more each and every time

He rubs the medallion a little more each time
And convincingly reassures himself that
He is the rightful Regent
Protector of his nephew
Prince Xenophon.

But now Xenophon
Has become of age
For all wonder of the world
to perform and music to play onstage

and

…

I can't allow this to happen
To play, in this wicked world that is only serious
because of cruelty.

The sun goes up and the Prince
awakens to the haunting
sounds
Of burned leaves
That have fallen as ashes on his palace ground

Ready for him to sing words
to
but Xenophon no longer wishes to sing
A true dark song
however haunting it may be.

All the black ravens of death
have flown away
Seldom are they not here
the cruelty of the Leper King will make sure that
they stay
Together with his madness!

THE DEATH OF ADONYS

A loud sound from Beirut shakes the palace to its core, breaking all its windows, even though the palace is miles away from the city. As if to say that all the voices of traumas in the world united and conspired to be heard in this explosion. An explosion which is still a phenomenon to the world, but all too familiar in Beirut and the world of Luciferous. Alarmed the king selfishly rushes out of the throne room to hide in the safety of his palace room, not thinking of anyone but himself. A room that Xenophon describes that on appearance it may be impressive and aesthetically beautiful, but felt like no more than a cold dungeon on the inside.

When the birds started chirping once more and the smoke cleared, a servant went to Xenophon's room, but found his chamber empty. The servant went to tell the king
'Sire your nephew isn't in his chambers!'
'Where is he!' The king yells in a manner that he is entitled to the world for answers
as though the world owed him everything including and especially power. Power to control the destinies of others.

The servant asks the guards where Xenophon went and who allowed him to leave. The man to betray Adonys, the leader of the order of guards, was done none other than by the person right underneath Adonys in the hierarchy of guards at least. His name was Jakob, and he snitched. The fate of Adonys was swiftly decided in front of the king's corrupt and wicked jury, and he was quickly rushed to behind the palace and hanged as a criminal,
hanged for Treason for conspiring to overthrow King Salazar I,

a sad injustice to dreamers such as Adonys
dreamers who dream of changing the currents
streams
of this world

This was all done before Xenophon eye's, whose eyes were forever changed after the killing of the Head of the Guards, after the murder of his favourite and most trusted uncle one best of the Order of Palace Guards.

OUR PHOENIX MAYAR

Upon learning of the murder of his uncle
of the murder of Adonys
A teary-eyed Xenophon walks up
to the legendary statues
where King Hector I's golden finger
touched the beak of the Phoenix
He imitates the touch of this Great King
and says
'O what flights of the Angel
Our Mayar (who my mother was daughter of)
Our immortal phoenix
Who has flown away from the carnage of our lands'?

Xenophon pauses and gazes at the fine features of
this statue
with its strong golden wings that encircle
The figure of our Great King Hector I
petting this fearless creature of beauty
a spectacle for all to watch

Her hot fires wrestled and caged in by the stillness
of her beauty
'Gone is Mayar, long has she left these lands
but not lost

I carry her hope for all men
For all Orentis

The cruelty of this king, a son of the Great King
Hector I,
has soiled this divine seat
and look set for making
a dynasty of imposters to the throne.

TASTE OF REVOLUTION

When the eye of the of a storm subdues
calmness ensues
and the idea of revolution pursues.

I have gone into Beirut
Ready to give everything
Left Beirut with everything
and a taste of ideas
Ideas of change
The city is circular
Circular as the Cerebrum
that must be shared
But is wedged by my uncle
Salazar the evil,
Who distributes the coin as he calls it
To himself and his cronies
Drunk on greed.

I must share
and exceed
In the need to share this mineral
So that the kingdom of Orentis
will no longer bleed
As it does as Luciferous.

But who will heed
Who will heed a man who
A man who is but a droplet sliding of a plant of weed?
Beirut is the ocean
Her waves and currents
Are the seeds of life
and her people the fish
Wish to not be served on a dish
By the imposter King.

With my trusted friends
I go back to the castle to challenge
And fight for what's mine by right!

To fight for
The throne!!

THE FLOWER IS ON THE TABLE

As the storm in Beirut
I charge into the
the Throne Room

where the seat of power resides
But ominously enough
my uncle is not there.

There is where the rose is placed
this flower on the table
confined by glass
elevate by the table
this hierarchy of a platform
and
The falling of her rose petals
To the violent rumbles outside
Whose flirtation pauses the gazes of all storms
For just a second
Its perfection seen through my eyes
All wonder from the thunder
outside
And the
Anger from its plunder
Anger from the injustice

You and I
To the God of death
Are but mortal men
Doomed to die

All men must die
And cry to the sound of music
To the sound of the explosion
Her songs of malice
So terrific

and
to the droplets from that cry
do we walk down
The straight line
3 6 9
Seconds into the new world
That the old world
Her order beckons
so as history would have it

that
one eyelid shuts
Another opens
To take one into the deep
ends of oceans

Decisions to be made
Blue skies that aid
Which order do we seek to trade?
One that allows you to get paid
Or one that allows you to be satisfied from the beauty
that you make,
As I start to awake all all the riddles
Start to look fake,

And I Xenophon nephew of the king,
and
Heir to the throne,
My rightful throne has been taken into the dungeons,
After rushing over.

And they killed him!
The king killed his little brother
for telling me the truth
of Luciferous' true origins,
they have killed him
they have killed my uncle
The King has killed his little brother
the Prince Adonys.

WRITER ON THE STORM

Xenophon is seen mounting a horse
To leave the throne room and
go
go back to Beirut
but
before he leaves
on his quest for seizure of the throne
He is seized by the revolutionary guards
loyal to king Salazar
But
how in the Devil did he know that he was there?

Thus, Xenophon's fight against the kingdom's
depression
from a prison cell begins.

It is a cold and singular fight,
depression is always lonely and cold
but thawed by the magic of fire,
magic which Xenophon possess.

Oddity from dark Clouds
group around before
the answer to the riddle is ushered in.

Malice on the streets
Those streets
famous streets before shroud by the infamous palace
Are remembered
and meant to be remembered
as places which filled hearts with joy and heat.

Now with this blistering coldness in the air
one can find that the only heat is in
the tension that runs deep
and poison from the Crown to the tyrannical King
extended throughout the whole kingdom of
Luciferous.

and a rift is created
this wedge between
Monarchy and people,
that separates them from the Cerebrum
found in the mine.

Beirut's beauty
whose society is punished for their heresy
by this port explosion
is a victim of the age
and tensions caused by Salazar's reign
just scratch the surface of problems.

The old order says that,
the skies darken
Where there is penance and rejection,
but the old order also says that
the skies turn blue when there is acceptance with the
antics of progression.

Luciferous's curse and world will only end and turn
green with progression
that can only be ushered in when
there is love between man and people
when the mine no longer continues to be a wedge
And reason for aggression
brought in from paranoia and fear
from the pendulum of power
which deems who controls
that mine and sits on the Luciferian throne.

They say that the Gods animates the world
With the sun and the moon,
that there is lightness and darkness
kept in balance
by the force of nature.

a writers animate the world
By their pains,
Use their depression to make drama.

Such a pity
that the fiery fuel
used to crackle their own worlds to motion
is from the judgements of people
and their worlds created from the oceans of people's
emotions.

For the Gods create all,
and all are not man made
Save for icy depressions
Singular in form
whose only solution to all
is to love the crackle of fire
but also to fight the fire
With the compassionate waters
of consciousness.

THE UPSIDE-DOWN KING

Shortly afterwards the police
assault Prince Xenohphon.

and escourt him to the ship waiting at the iconic port,
barren and destroyed by the blast.

Orders by
my uncle
the king
this unjust king!

And with the cards of succession dashed aside
I feel helpless
possessed by madness
from my failed attempt of running
running to you
the crown!
I guess that
the real curse is running in a race that is a reverse,
one never has a conversation in a Race
just talk that becomes evil
and
evil is upside down.

Evil is his crown,
I feel the victim's sting
of being the upside-down baffled king,
the pain of the world
brought in by the rain
falling onto the dungeon,
tickling the heads of other prisoners
my friends who helped me assault the throne,
for crimes of treason
locked in this old ship
sailing away into the horizon
far from the bay
where my uncle the king reigns.

Banished and locked in,
I am beside my prisoner's meal,
counting my sins and finding
no wrong in attempting to assume a throne
that was rightfully mine in the first place—
or should I have remained a sheep
destined to follow,
only to be served and eaten as lamb
on a prisoner's tray?

Cruel whispers from people who call themselves friends
and the bitter symphony from squeaking
mice trod around me,
scheming for their reward

in our shared darkness,
locked up together,
men and mice wishing to rise—
but our struggles are not the same.

The unfairness of the dice cast,
man is chained to his past,
no rules to guide this game of chance
in this dark dungeon called life.

Man, the maker
waits for the golden wings of destiny
to change bitter realities
and fly up with the children of the skies.

Yet to be born with royal blood
is too heavy for such dangly wings.
The gravity of power is unbearable,
its curse irreversible.
A king was slain
Xenophon's father,
his heir now caged,
doomed to the roll of the dice
which says that he should breathe the same air as
the mice.

STILL WATER

The ship carrying these prisoners leaves Beirut
from the same port that exploded.
Xenophon reflects as he stares into the fountain
before he is locked up in his dungeon cell
and
where he was a freeman before.
and he stares into the placid pond
So still when juxtaposed to the turbulent waters,
flowing from the fountain's mouth
and ponders at the point
Where each king would go to
to stare into waters
and find his own
reflection
and ponder of what's wrong in that opposite world
even if it is to remind them of
how they look like
with or without the crown,
reflect upon those years
of glory
and find comfort
as those moths in my prison do to my prison cell flame
comfort in worlds that are victim to tragedies bending
of the light
the sky

the sky is polite
when it cloaks the world
and tucks in its people
in the moments after the day has burned into the
cold night,
and wait in the dying hours of the black night
for the futures promise
of
Tomorrow
…
for people
burdened with troubles of power
power burdened with light
light that instantly triumphs over darkness,
for tomorrow is never drowned by darkness
the great artist of this world
does spare the brush
of power to be shared
between sun and moon.
That I, Xenophon should stare into the pool to find
back my reflection
and conclude to my bloodied self
that
Power in the hands of humans
at the end of the day is a lens
a lens that is worn by one
at the other's expense
ideas were never the race.

and the reflection of the castle behind
is a kingdom unrecognised by me
it is a kingdom lost to paradise
It is Beirut!
and I must do well to jump her
hurdle made of wood
and wood can be burned,
I commence intent on beginning my own reign
The Reign of the Phoenix.
Prison and the Horizon
'The ship has just left its harbour
from my prison cell
beyond the fountains well
I can see the horizon
see the sun set in the west,
I will land wherever the sun rises in the East
a ship made of invincible steel
I look back at the pond and reflect
on my own light
and seldom see any shadows.
indeed, immortality brings the beauty of life without
the sadness of death,
it is just infinite life with no end, but what it is life
without death?
The cycle of life must have death as must the cycle of
death must have life.
The tragedy of life is that there must be a balance
between life and death

Power at each of the cycle's end must be shared.
I am a man reborn! Reborn from the flames
ready to fight in this game of thorns.
Ready to begin
with the rising sun of the East
begin my reign
the Reign of the Phoenix
and set in the West.'

Printed in Great Britain
by Amazon

79490705R00107